Diary of A Stepfather
Leslie Wilson

An Extended Case Study

**Foreword by
Margaret Robinson**

Published by
STEPFAMILY Publications

The National Stepfamily Association

© 1996 NATIONAL STEPFAMILY ASSOCIATION

ISBN 1 873309 20 1

All rights reserved. No part of this publication may be reproduced, stored in a retrieval system or transmitted in any form or by any means, electronic, mechanical. photocopying, recording or otherwise without the prior permission of the publisher.

Published by STEPFAMILY Publications
National Stepfamily Association
Chapel House, 18 Hatton Place
London EC1N 8RU
Registered Charity No 1005351
Company Limited by guarantee No 2552166

Telephone: 0171 209 2460 (office)
             0990 168 388 (Counselling line)

Printed by Lonsdale Press
Designed by STEPFAMILY

Acknowledgements

In 1994, the National Stepfamily Association and Families at Risk marked the International Year of the Family by jointly hosting a two day conference on "Successful Stepfamilies UK 1994: Everyday realities, risks and protective factors."

One of the presentations, by Margaret Robinson, focused on the impact of former marriages on stepfamilies and drew on current therapeutic work within her practice. She obtained permission from one of her clients to read from a diary he had begun in an attempt to understand the transformation for him of moving from his first marriage to a stepfamily.

This publication arises from the continuing therapeutic work around his diary.

We are enormously grateful to Leslie for having written so frankly and movingly about the difficult transitions and adjustments he has made and observed in others. We are also grateful to Leslie's network of family and stepfamily (all the names within this publication have been changed to protect confidentiality) for enabling us to learn more about the impact of family change through his experiences with them.

Finally, we are grateful to the Department of Health who contributed to the cost of this, our second, publication on the role of stepfathering

Dedicated to
'Jenny'

Contents

Acknowledgements	3
Foreword	7
June 1994	11
August 1994	18
November 1994	24
January 1995	26
February 1995	32
March 1995	35
April 1995	38
Easter 1995	40
October 1995	42
January 1996	50
Afterword	52
Useful Books	53
Useful Addresses	54

Foreword

When I suggested to Leslie that he might write a diary for himself in order to explore his experience of living with his new partner, I little thought that I would subsequently be asked to write this foreword. However, I am now delighted to do so as Leslie has written so poignantly and honestly about the situation in which he found himself. I have met many men who have experienced the deep pain which he describes but have found considerable difficulty in articulating it. I hope this published version of his diary may help those who read it make more sense of their own situation, both to recognise their pain and find ways of managing it which are healing, rather than destructive of themselves or others.

At the time I made this suggestion to Leslie, I was seeing him and his new partner Jenny in order to help them with some of the difficulties in their relationship and their stepfamily situation. He always discussed his diary entries with her and sometimes sent me copies a few days in advance so that at our relatively infrequent meetings we could discuss them, together with other issues which they both raised.

Like many fathers who leave a marriage which no longer sufficiently meets their needs, Leslie neither wanted to abandon his child, nor absolve himself of responsibility for the financial care of his then wife Teressa. For him the greatest loss through his divorce was that of his day to day relationship with his son, Thomas then aged 8. As the diary shows, Leslie felt he had missed out on a close relationship with his own father, who emigrated after he and his mother divorced. Like many present day fathers he had determinedly built a close and loving relationship with Thomas.

Leslie had met Jenny, also a partner in what was for her an unfulfilling marriage, and they began what became a mutually loving relationship, something which neither of them had. Although like many mothers in deeply unhappy relationships she had left the matrimonial home, she had not abandoned her children, returning to attend to their needs and generally to continue their care. She and her husband Adrian attended mediation and subsequently it was agreed that he would leave the matrimonial home. She would return, so that the children could stay in their home, having their mother's daily presence and care and seeing their father by arrangement. As Leslie seems to demonstrate, Adrian took longer to come to terms with the divorce and may have used the children to meet the needs of his own loneliness rather than creating a firm but flexible structure for them. Teressa would not agree to attend mediation and as the diary shows Leslie struggled hard and painfully to maintain his loving relationship with his son.

In moving in with Jenny and her children, Leslie not only gave up his own home, but also, perhaps out of guilt for abandoning his former wife, gave her an excessive amount of maintenance from his income, thus not only living in Jenny's home in a small village, but also rendering him disproportionately financially dependent on her. Jenny and her children already had a familiar way of day to day living in their home together, and as all families do had their own set of family rules. Both Leslie and Jenny wanted to maintain these, but were surprised and hurt when this made difficulties within their relationship.

As the diary shows, like all stepfamilies, it was very hard for them to have their own 'private space' which also made it difficult for them to resolve the problems which inevitably arose. This is a common problem for stepfamilies, particularly those who feel guilty about initially putting their own needs above those of the children. They then often overcompensate by not taking sufficient time to nourish their own relationship, itself an important alternative model for both sets of children who have already experienced the breakdown (or loss) of the relationship of their birth parents.

As children usually live with their mothers post-separation and divorce, most full-time stepfamilies are stepfather households, in which the mother is considered the residential parent. Leslie and Jenny's family could therefore be described as customary in this way, just as would Leslie in the language of the Child Support Act be considered as the 'absent parent', which he certainly had no wish to be. Their family circumstances again are not unusual, Leslie moved into Jenny's family home and territory which as he describes, made difficulties for her as well as for him. Secondly, and about which he writes so vividly, he moved into a family which was already coping with adolescent children, which as the father of Thomas, he had not yet directly experienced himself. This confronted them both with problems difficult enough and more usually faced by both biological parents, rather than a parent and stepparent. Building relationships with stepchildren is never easy and takes time and patience. Leslie writes of his feelings of jealousy and irritation, particularly of his stepdaughter Rachel.

The difficulties of what could be described as jumping into a later stage of the family life cycle is more usually faced by stepmothers, who as Donna Smith writes in her book on "Stepmothering" (Harvester Wheatsheaf, 1990) often also have to face this in a part-time stepfamily.

But this is already long enough as an introduction to Leslie's diary and I will commend it to the reader not only for its openness, courage and honesty in revealing what is difficult for many men, but because it is also lucidly written.

Margaret Robinson,
Stepparent, marital and family therapist and mediator.
April 1996

Diary of a Stepfather: An Extended Case Study

June 1994

I am writing this in June 1994, shortly after I moved in to live with Jenny and her children. The last year has been traumatic, painful, exciting and enlivening.

In July 1993 we both left our partners after years of marriage: 16 in my case, 22 in Jenny's. Teressa and I have a son, Thomas, aged 8. Jenny and Adrian have three children - Peter, 19, Roger, 15 and Rachel, 13.

The decision to leave was painful for both of us. I still find it hard to think back to the day I left, in particular Thomas hanging on to my legs, pleading with me not to leave. I remember saying to Jenny shortly before we left that if we were to do it we should hold hands and both jump. On several occasions over the following months we said that if we had known how hard it was going to be we probably would not have taken the same decision. Certainly I feel that whatever the rights and wrongs of what we have done, we took a bold, courageous step; in many ways it would have been easier and safer to have stayed.

After several nights together in a farmhouse bed and breakfast we moved into a rented house. I had anticipated that it would be hard learning to live together after so many years of living with another partner - in fact, it proved surprisingly easy. Of course, there were some adjustments to make: the first trip to Sainsbury's provoked several cries of 'What on earth is that? I'm not eating that!' Our first holiday together was delayed by problems in packing: we both sat around waiting for the other to pack, as had happened in our marriages. But generally it was easy for us to be together.

I have happy memories of those early months together. We had lots of time to get to know each other and relatively few outside demands on us. Thus we were able to go for long walks together, go to the opera, eat out and generally enjoy being together. We were also able to spend a lot of time in bed, holding and touching each other, talking and making love. This was a luxury which was extremely valuable to us. It was a freedom which we both miss now that we are living with Jenny's children.

Alongside this love and enjoyment of each other there were also many painful areas. I missed Thomas terribly. I had always spent a lot of time with him and been very involved with him. I had had a very poor relationship with my own father who had been absent for most of my childhood and who died when I was in my early twenties. It had therefore been extremely important to me to be a good father to Thomas and to give him the paternal love which I had missed so much. In leaving Teressa I had wondered whether I was unconsciously repeating the same pattern as my father and abandoning Thomas as I had been abandoned.

I was lucky in the sense that Thomas made it very clear that he wanted to see me regularly and spend time with me. However, he was also very angry with me and expressed this openly. He frequently used to ask me whether I loved Jenny more than him and would not accept it when I told him that the love was different. We have always had a physical relationship and in those days he would 'play fight' with me in an extremely rough and aggressive manner. He also initially said that he would never want to meet Jenny.

I also felt considerable guilt and concern in relation to Teressa. I was left with a curious sense of paradox: on the one hand the feeling that I had done a terrible thing by inflicting so much pain on Teressa and Thomas; on the other a sense of 'rightness' about being with Jenny. It was frequently hard to reconcile these two feelings. Indeed, it felt so 'right' to be with Jenny that I almost found it hard to understand why Teressa was so distressed and angry.

For both Jenny and I there began the long process of letting go of and mourning our marriages. While I did not miss Teressa, I felt desperately sad about the end of my marriage. I can remember about three months after leaving being deeply moved by a beautiful drawing of a mother, father and their baby. I am still carrying a sense of failure about the breakdown of my marriage and the ideal of the 'happy family'.

At the same time Jenny was struggling with intense feelings of guilt and sadness. Her husband put considerable pressure on her to return to him and she had to endure some very painful criticism from her family. On several occasions I think she came close to going back to him. While I could understand this from an intellectual point of view, I also felt enormously hurt by it and angry with her.

It felt to me that we needed to forgive ourselves for what we had done and give ourselves permission to be happy. In particular, it felt like we needed to allow ourselves to be happy when our ex-partners were not.

After several months the situation changed when Jenny and Adrian reached an agreement whereby she spent half of the week back at her house looking after her children. After a long and bitter struggle, Adrian finally moved out of the house in January 1994 and Jenny moved back in full time.

I had mixed feelings about all this. Partly I felt that it was more difficult for Jenny to end her marriage than me - how does a woman end her marriage without either abandoning her children or throwing her husband out of his house? Interestingly, Jenny came in for more severe criticism than I did and it felt as though society is more tolerant of a man ending a marriage than of a woman. At the same time I also felt that Jenny, perhaps out of guilt, colluded with Adrian, gave him confusing messages and offered him some hope that she might return to him. It still feels now as though Jenny is protective of him and does not recognise when he is being manipulative and playing on her guilt. I also felt that the need to continue the parental relationship makes it much harder to end the emotional, romantic relationship. Perhaps slightly cynically, I believe that Adrian uses issues around the children and contact with them as a way of retaining some emotional dependence on Jenny - contact is never straightforward or in a routine, with the result that Adrian and Jenny seem to need to renegotiate it every week.

At the same time my guilt has caused problems in relation to Teressa and Thomas. I have probably been paying Teressa more maintenance than I can afford. I have found it very difficult to be clear about this and Jenny might say that I have been weak. In the process I have been putting Jenny in a difficult position and taken advantage of her generosity.

In relation to Thomas, my guilt has led to a temptation to buy him lots of presents and give him treats. It has also meant that I have found it difficult to be firm with him: for some months I let him get away with things which I would never have previously allowed. Thomas tended to play on this, several times saying that he would not come to see me unless I agreed to a particular demand. I was aware that I quickly lost confidence in dealing with him and felt very out of touch with him.

My guilt, lack of self-confidence and the problems of facing up to Teressa and Thomas' continuing hostility all made me appreciate why so many fathers disappear from their children's lives. While I know that Thomas needs me to remain in close contact and continue to absorb his anger, this also feels difficult and painful for me. My father reacted to his situation by moving to the USA and beginning a completely new life there; for the first time I could understand and identify with him.

With Jenny moving back to her children I had to cope with my jealousy of them and the necessity to share her with them. This has applied particularly with Rachel, who has needed a lot of time with Jenny and who has been especially distressed by her parents' separation. This whole aspect feels a bit easier now, but there were many times in the past when I resented Jenny's children and wished that she did not have any. Thus I have had to learn to cope with Jenny as a mother as well as my partner, and accept that there are going to be times when she will spend time with them rather than me. Thomas is 8 and I feel relatively comfortable and confident with his age group. But teenagers seem completely different and in many ways I think I am out of touch with them. I had not realised how noisy teenagers are (music, television, shouting, etc.) or how quickly their moods change.

From January onwards I gradually began spending more time at Jenny's house, sleeping overnight from February onwards. I initially had to face a certain amount of hostility from Rachel and Roger: Rachel several times told Jenny that if I ever moved in she would move out. It has been very hard to balance the children's needs for time and space with our own impatience and desire to be together. We have had to give Peter, Roger and Rachel time to mourn their parents' separation without giving them the feeling of being in control of making major decisions. I also found this period difficult as I was living half the week at Jenny's house and the other half in a flat: I felt very rootless. In the event I moved in permanently in the middle of June.

The first few days were very awkward for me and I felt ill at ease with Jenny's children, struggling to believe that I had a right to be in their house. Jenny seemed to cope easily initially, but then hit a crisis after about a week. She suddenly became angry with me and questioned whether she wanted me to be at the house. I felt very vulnerable, wanting to negotiate some sort of contract; at least with the estate agents I had to be given a month's notice in writing! However, Jenny's doubts soon passed and we both overcame our initial panic. In fact, writing this three weeks after moving in I have been surprised at how easy the process has been - Jenny's children have been much more accepting of me than I anticipated and it has been wonderful for Jenny and me to be together all the time. No doubt there will be many problems and issues to come, but thus far our main feeling has been happiness at being together. Perhaps also Jenny's children sense how much happier their mother is now and they are responding to her greater contentment.

The last thought has helped me in terms of my role: at times I have felt that with my own ambivalence about teenagers I have very little to offer them. However, I have come to feel that through loving Jenny and helping her to be more at peace I can indirectly offer them something which will benefit them.

Some issues remain around money, and this is still the area

about which we have most difficulty in communicating. Jenny's standard of living is higher than I have been used to and this can make me feel awkward. Although we have agreed a monthly figure which I pay Jenny, she is being heavily penalised financially in terms of maintenance by my presence in the house. She probably also feels that I am subsidising Teressa's extravagance at her expense. For myself, my pride is hurt by the fact that Jenny has so much more money than I have and that my financial situation is such a mess. I feel caught between my guilt in relation to Teressa, my desire to provide consistency for Thomas in terms of where he lives, and Jenny's justified (but annoying!) feeling that I am undervaluing myself and penalising her in the process. Right now it feels as though my financial situation will take a long time to resolve.

In terms of my role and relationship with Peter, Roger and Rachel, this is still difficult at times. At present I keep out of any conflicts between Jenny and her children, but it is very tempting to jump in and take sides. In my work I have recently come across two reconstituted families in which the 'stepfather' has very quickly taken on an authoritarian and disciplinary role - this feels very inappropriate for me, although at times understandable in terms of my wish to have some power and control in the situation. Certainly, it seems to me that currently in society there is considerable confusion and uncertainty about what fathers 'do'. This confusion is even more of an issue with stepfathers.

August 1994

Writing this two months after moving in, I feel that I have just come through a very difficult phase. I suddenly feel a renewal of my love for Jenny and a much greater sense of relaxation about being here. Quite how this has happened I am not clear - a few weeks ago I was tense, nervous and on edge about being here. It has felt to me as though Jenny has no idea how hard it is to move into someone else's house and adjust to their way of life: she has been impatient with my depression and expected me to adjust quickly. I have resented the fact that I am the one having to make all the adjustments. In many ways Jenny and her children's lives have not altered that dramatically (at least in a practical, routine sense) - I am the one who has adjusted and learnt to fit in to their routines.

I also continue to miss Thomas and find this hard to adjust to: on the one hand I enjoy the greater freedom this brings me and the increased time I have; on the other I miss the sense of being a 'day-to-day' dad. This has left a gap in my life and a need to redefine who I am as a person. Previously being a father and a protective carer to Teressa gave me a sense of role and made me feel useful and important. Now I have to find a way of being a father when I only see Thomas twice a week. I also have to find a way of being which does not depend solely on being a father and protector.

This is significant in terms of my relationship with Jenny. One of the differences for me is that I feel a much greater sense of equality and mutuality. With Jenny I am not always the protector or carer but we can take it in turns to be vulnerable, needy, etc.; my needs can also be met.

However, I have recently become aware again of the necessity to keep communicating. Recently while I was struggling here I became withdrawn and less communicative. This, in turn, had an effect on our relationship, particularly on our sex life. In part, this has felt connected to being here: with Jenny's children around it is often not easy to have healthy conflict and settle our disputes. We have prided ourselves on being able to talk through difficult, painful issues in a way which neither of us could do in our marriages. This has felt more difficult over the past few months and has highlighted the need for us to have time and space together away from the children.

It has also been interesting for me to observe the effect of lack of communication on our relationship and I felt much less close to Jenny when I was holding on to my feelings; I have learnt again how damaging unexpressed feelings can be. One of the things I love about Jenny is her resilience and toughness, and it has been wonderful for me to (play) fight with her in a way which I could never do with Teressa. I also realise now how one of the most damaging aspects of my marriage was the years' worth of feelings, anger, resentment, etc. which I did not express directly.

It has proved difficult for Jenny and I to keep some space for our own relationship. At times this has been an issue between us as Jenny has been keen not to make her children feel excluded. Looking after our relationship without pushing away the children has seemed a difficult balance. This has been a problem because of the children's erratic contact with Adrian. We had assumed that they would be staying regularly with him, but Roger in particular has been reluctant to stay there and it has not happened nearly as often as we had anticipated. They also often go over to Adrian's individually (Adrian seems to prefer this) and at times it seems like they go over by rota so that one of them is always here. This has created some problems for our sexual relationship. When we were living in our house together we would frequently spend the afternoon in bed. I really valued this and loved being able to spend hours in bed together. This has proved impossible to do here and has caused me considerable frustration. Often in the evenings we will say to each other, 'What is the earliest we can go to bed?' (without the children thinking we are going to bed to make love; which of course we are).

There has also been a major issue over our bedroom. In the past the children have been in the habit of using the telephone and the bathroom in Jenny and Adrian's bedroom. This has been very difficult for me - several times I have gone up to the bedroom wanting a bit of peace and quiet to find one of the children talking on the phone. This has created some tension between Jenny and myself: I want to create a space for us which is separate from the children, she does not want to push them out.

As part of this process, we have fitted a lock on our bedroom door which has also led to some tension. Recently I was giving Jenny a back massage in our bedroom with the door locked. Rachel tried to come in and was angry and upset to find the door locked - the back massage ended speedily! This all feels like part of the difficulty we have in acknowledging in a public way that we have a sexual relationship and that we need space and time on our own away from the children. I guess that it is made more difficult by the fact that Roger and Rachel are teenagers and are beginning to get in touch with their own sexuality.

I also find it hard when Jenny spends a lot of time with her children. Partly this is my envy and resentment that she still lives with her children and cares for them daily when I no longer live with Thomas. There are times when it feels as though I have had to make more sacrifices than Jenny and have lost more than she has. At such times I resent the children and the demands they make on Jenny.

This also tends to fuel my feelings that the children don't help around the house. This partly stems from my uncertainty about teenagers - I haven't got a clue how much teenagers normally do to help. In part also it connects with my feelings about Adrian. He used to work long hours and his attitude tended to be that he did the important business while Jenny did the minor things like bringing up the children; the message and expectation were that Jenny would deal with everything at home. This is not an attitude I feel comfortable with and it makes me angry on Jenny's behalf. In fact, Peter and Roger are not like this, but I think I have been on the lookout for any hint of this attitude in how they treat their mum. The fact that they don't do a lot (probably entirely normal for teenagers) raises fears in me that they will come to take on this expectation about women.

This has been one of the ways in which Adrian and Teressa's shadows continue to fall on our lives. Their impact has been particularly noticeable in relation to sex. Freud's comment that there are six people in the marital bed strikes me as a great understatement - often it seems to me as though there are six plus Adrian, Teressa and our four children!

Jenny and I made the decision that we would continue to live in her house. Partly this was because the children made it very clear that they wanted to remain in the house: their school is about half a mile away and they have lots of friends nearby. It seemed important to provide them with this continuity at a time when they had to cope with so much change. In addition, if we did move now I would not be able to contribute to buying a new house as I still have a joint mortgage with Teressa. It therefore seems more sensible to wait for a few years until the children have left school and my financial situation is (hopefully!) less of a mess. Jenny and I have both tried to make the house feel like 'ours': we have bought furniture together, installed my books in the study and changed our bedroom around. Despite this it is still difficult for me in a number of ways: it contributes to my feeling of following in Jenny's shadow, that she is the boss(!) and that I respond to her initiatives. And I think that issues around the bedroom partly reflect the fact that it used to be Adrian's bedroom.

Thomas now comes to the house regularly. His initial refusal to meet Jenny didn't last long and the two of them get on remarkably well. Recently we went to my mother's house for the day, which is just near the sea; I felt enormous happiness watching Jenny and Thomas play together in the sea, laughing and joking together. I have also made efforts to ensure that I spend time alone with Thomas, as this seems really important. Fortunately, we have a shared love of cricket and football which connects us.

It has been difficult for Peter, Roger, Rachel and Thomas to get to know each other. Thomas has been keen to get to know them, especially Peter and Roger whom he tends to look up to. The fact that Peter and Roger have a Sega Megadrive is a great attraction to Thomas and I'm sure he would really like to spend time with them. However, Roger in particular has been very cool with him - perhaps out of a fear that Thomas will never leave him alone if he gives him any encouragement! Initially I found this difficult: the first time Thomas came over Roger and Rachel scarcely spoke to him and I was angry and hurt for him. I remember thinking that I could cope with them being sullen with me but I would get very angry if they were stroppy with Thomas. At present he doesn't stay overnight and it is hard to know the best time to start this; right now it doesn't seem as though Roger and Rachel are ready for this yet. Until I feel more confident in the house it does not feel right to push this.

November 1994

The other night Jenny, Roger, Rachel and I went out for a meal together and then to the theatre. It was good to go out together and we all enjoyed it. While at the theatre we met a teacher from a local school. This teacher knows us both individually but did not know that we were living together. When I told her she reacted with great excitement and said how happy she was to hear the news. Later that night, Jenny commented that this was the first time someone had reacted with such joy at our coming together.

This was brought home to me the following day. While out in the car we saw a huge sign saying 'Congratulations Colin and Sally' (presumably on their wedding or engagement). It reminded me of the fact that usually when couples come together the reaction is one of joy and celebration. In contrast, the reaction to our relationship has varied from silence to overt criticism and disapproval. The criticisms have been compounded by our children's understandable anger and probable wish for our relationship to fail. These reactions have been very isolating and have put us in a lonely position. There have been times when I have almost felt ashamed of our relationship; rather than celebrate our love it has seemed necessary to hide it from the outside world. In some ways Jenny has found this harder to cope with than I have - partly because she has lived in this village (where she has been the object of strong disapproval) for several years and knows many more people than me; and partly because I am by nature more of a loner and a rebel. It is often said that stepfamilies are based on loss; in addition, our relationship is based on a considerable amount of hostility and disapproval.

This has relevance in terms of getting married (that is, if Jenny ever gets divorced!). There are many occasions when getting married seems unnecessary and unimportant. However, there are also times when it feels as though it would be good to have some sort of celebration and public declaration of our relationship. It seems crucial for Jenny and I to find a way of celebrating being together. I have suggested that we have a ritual way of commemorating the day of our first kiss, by buying each other a small gift.

January 1995

We have just survived our first Christmas together as a stepfamily. All told it went pretty well and it wasn't as difficult as I had imagined. However, it got off to a difficult beginning. I felt uncomfortable about three weeks before Christmas, as though I was having to make all the adjustments and fit into Jenny's routines about Christmas. As with most things, Jenny has very clear ideas about how Christmas should be celebrated, how decorations should be hung, etc. Next year I shall buy some decorations and introduce some of my own rituals about Christmas. Maybe my adjusting and fitting in was appropriate for this year, but in future I hope that Jenny and I will be able to develop some new rituals and traditions of our own. This is all part of an on-going dilemma: how much to respect past patterns, habits, traditions, etc. in order to provide continuity for the children; and how much to introduce new traditions to mark the fact that things have changed and moved on and we are now a different family.

I didn't see Thomas for two weeks over Christmas. He was going to stay here for the first time a couple of days before Christmas, but this didn't happen: partly because he was ill, and partly because I think Teressa did not want it to happen. The likelihood is that it will be some years before I see him on Christmas Day. It helps me to take a longer-term perspective on this. I tell myself that I shall be his father for the rest of my life and that we will have plenty of time together in future. Recently I saw a man of about my age sitting with an older man, who I assumed was his father, in a pub. They were talking happily together and clearly enjoying each other's company. I immediately envisaged sitting with

Thomas in a pub in 30 years' time, enjoying being together. I hope that in future we will be able to spend lots of time together to make up for what we are both missing out on now. This episode also made me think with sadness how much I would love to be able to go out to the pub with my father.

In the event, Thomas stayed for the first time after the New Year. He coped pretty well, seemed to enjoy himself and was intrigued by the early morning routines. I was extremely nervous. Partly I was afraid that if it did not go well he would not want to stay again; partly it now makes me miss him more and makes me sad and dissatisfied when I take him back to his home in the evenings. Predictably Teressa is not keen on his staying regularly - he will get too tired and be unable to cope with school.

On-going thoughts about stepfamilies: I don't feel anything like a parent to Peter, Roger and Rachel and I'm sure they do not see me in this way. Partly this is because of their ages and the fact that I do not feel ready to be in a parental role with teenagers; and partly because it feels much too early to take on this sort of role. In fact, I now get on quite well with all three of them, but I think that this is precisely because I do not take on a parental role. For instance, Roger, who has exams later this year, is put under a lot of pressure by his mum and dad to work harder. He often seems relieved that I don't get into any of this but instead talk about football or juggling. It certainly feels as though they are not ready to accept me as a parental figure; and certainly Thomas is not ready to accept Jenny.

I have several times read that traditional gender roles don't work in stepfamilies. I have recently witnessed this in my work with a stepfamily involving a mother, stepfather and two girls aged six and three. The stepfather comes from Portugal and his understanding of being 'father' means that he has taken on a strong, disciplinary parental role from an early stage. His understanding of families leads him to see himself as the head of the family unit. This is clearly resented by the six-year-old girl and I foresee many conflicts: 'You can't tell me what to do - you aren't my father!'

Our experience has taught us the need to be much more flexible in our roles and generally Jenny looks after and deals with her children while I care for Thomas. However, major readjustments have also been necessary. It seems to me as though Jenny and Adrian had a very traditional marriage, with Adrian working and Jenny looking after the home and the family. Jenny acted as the central person through whom everyone else communicated: there are times when Rachel will ask Jenny what Roger is doing or what he means even when he is in the room. It has often felt to me as though Adrian is unused to communicating directly with the children and tries to communicate with them via Jenny. This has been particularly evident over contact. For a long time Adrian and the children seemed unable to sort out between them when contact would happen and they all looked to Jenny to organise it. Adrian used Jenny a bit like a secretary: he would give her a list of his available dates and expect her to organise the contact from that. I was unhappy about this, feeling that it was time Adrian grew up and that it put Jenny in an impossible position. Now she has withdrawn from this role, but it means that contact is haphazard, erratic and unpredictable.

Another readjustment has been that Jenny has had to take on responsibility for thinking about and organising money in a way which she never previously had to. She also has more responsibility for the maintenance of the house and finds this stressful. This can sometimes lead to conflict between us: it feels to me as though Jenny wants to be in control of this house, do everything her way and so on, until something goes wrong whereupon she expects me to sort it out instantly. Jenny has just read this, thinks I am being unfair (which I probably am) and wants me to rewrite it (which I won't).

I believe that one of the reasons for things working reasonably well is that I have fitted into the routines of the house. In many ways this means that things have carried on for Roger and Rachel as they were in the past. Clearly there have been lots of changes, but in a practical, routine way there has been a sense of continuity for them. Similarly, Jenny now runs the house in the same way she always has. While this continuity has been important for Roger and Rachel, it is often hard for me. I still feel as though this is not really my house and I sometimes resent the fact that I have made so many changes while Jenny's life has carried on pretty much as before. I deliberately have not made many demands for myself, feeling that it is important for Roger and Rachel that familiar routines are followed. I guess that it would be very different if Jenny and I did not have children. I would then feel much freer about arguing with her and re-establishing our own joint way of doing things.

Yesterday I felt particularly miserable and lonely. I strongly wanted to go home, some place where I feel safe, except I do not know where 'home' is. I suddenly feel homeless and rootless. It seems strange that I should be like this after a good Christmas and a much easier period with Roger and Rachel. Partly I think that it is because I feel threatened by any change. It feels as though I have had so many changes over the past two years that I can't cope with any more. I now have a new boss at work and am finding this a very difficult adjustment. And the office is being reorganised in a way which will change my job slightly. In the past I would have coped with this much more easily, but now I feel threatened and frightened by it all.

I am also feeling criticised and attacked a lot. Thomas is still angry with me and frequently has a go at me. He is often affectionate with me but alternates this with criticism. He remains fiercely loyal to Teressa and always attacks me if I am in conflict with her (which he always seems to know about, not from me). Currently Teressa and I are arguing about money - she is wanting me to pay her legal bill of £1600, which is difficult as I only have savings of £400. Last night Thomas asked me how much money I pay to Teressa. When I refused to tell him he said, 'Probably not very much, you are so mean.' I feel very hurt by these attacks and feel a strong temptation to criticise his mother and tell him that she is not so perfect. I am also angry that she finds a way of involving him in our disputes and that he gets caught up in things which he should not know about. This has the effect of inhibiting me from getting involved in conflicts with Teressa. In terms of valuing myself and standing up for my rights, it feels important that I confront Teressa about certain issues, for instance money and Thomas staying with me. However, I know that if I do this Thomas will get to hear about it and will attack me. My fear is that my relationship with him will suffer.

I also miss him a lot and find it hard being a dad when I only see him twice a week. It is often hard to take his anger without retaliating. It is also hard to keep in touch with him and how he is changing. At Christmas I found it difficult to know what to buy him. Recently he showed me one of his school reading books and I was amazed at how advanced it was - I had no idea that his reading had become that good.

The temptation is to continue to treat him as he was at the time I left, whereas in reality he has moved on enormously since then. Another point is that I sometimes feel inhibited from telling what I am doing for fear that he will immediately tell Teressa. I have no wish for her to know about my life, but it seems important for Thomas to be involved. He is also very secretive about many aspects of his life and if I ask him he often says, 'Wouldn't you like to know?'

Added to this is the fact that I am being criticised a lot in my work at present. The job is stressful, often dealing with angry and disturbed people. I have too much to do, with the result that there are some things which remain undone. It feels like a struggle to cope and my motivation is currently low.

A further stress is that Jenny and I have recently had birthdays. Roger and Rachel seemed to cope with this well, giving me a present and being friendly with me. However, Thomas was not so happy and became jealous of Jenny. He several times asked me whether I preferred his or Jenny's present and he did not want me to spend any time with her on her birthday. I felt torn between Thomas and Jenny, as though I had to make a choice between them. He was also quite stroppy with Jenny on her birthday and hardly spoke to her.

February 1995

Thomas continues to be angry with me and Jenny and I am puzzled why this is happening now - not so long ago he seemed to be coping well, whereas now he is much more angry. He is also having far less to do with Jenny and he is clearly angry with her. He told me the other day that he was angry with her because she had taken me away from Teressa. It is curious that this is happening now. I do wonder whether it is a reaction to his staying overnight - although he seemed to cope OK at the time.

On Saturday he was particularly grumpy and bad tempered. I was also in a bad mood and didn't much enjoy having him here. After he had gone I felt angry with myself for not enjoying his presence and I began missing him again. Only seeing him twice a week brings a pressure to make the most of those times in an artificial way. I now feel that I would like to see him more and have more 'normal' time with him. Teressa remains opposed to his staying during term time and was also not keen when I proposed taking him away on holiday over the summer. She refuses to talk at length about any of this and will not go to mediation. Thomas' anger and upset have confronted me a bit more about his and Teressa's feelings. I think that over the past 18 months I have been absorbed with my own feelings and have not felt so much about Thomas and Teressa's. I guess that this is partly because of my guilt and the pain of facing up to their distress. Certainly it is really hard to hear Thomas' pain and anger.

I had a dream about Teressa last night. It was in her house and she had left messages around saying that she was going to kill herself. Then she began dancing very provocatively, with her nipples coming out through holes in her clothes.

I've been thinking about her more recently. The dream reminds me of when I told her I was leaving: she tried stuffing some tablets in her mouth and screamed and cried for about 20 minutes. I held and restrained her during this time. Thomas was around, obviously very scared and at one point said to me, 'If Mummy dies will you look after me?'

Teressa remains very angry with me. She rarely looks me in the eyes; when she does it is with a look which says that she will never forgive me. I am left with lots of contradictory feelings: the sense that I have done a terrible thing to her (divorce is a polite form of murder, as I read once) and yet the awareness that I am happier now and much more intimate with Jenny than I could ever have been with Teressa. I know that if I had stayed I would only have lived half a life.

I am struck again by how differently Jenny and I have handled the situation. Jenny has spent quite a bit of time talking to Adrian, knows a lot about his life now and how he is feeling. Teressa and I have hardly spoken except about Thomas and I know very little about her life. She has refused to go to any kind of mediation and I am left with a sense of lots of things unsaid and unspoken. It also feels as though I have reacted against my father (I have spent a lot of my life trying to be the opposite of my father). He was indecisive and came and went for several years; in contrast I acted decisively, perhaps brutally and very quickly. I probably also made it clear to her that I was not prepared to listen to her grief and anger. I feel as though I am just beginning to face up to some of the sadness. I don't miss her and still feel a sense of relief. But now I am feeling sadder again about my marriage. Perhaps the hassles around seeing Thomas and around money have made it harder for me to acknowledge my sadness.

March 1995

Thomas stayed again over half-term and seemed to enjoy being here. He has been less aggressive with Jenny lately and more affectionate with me. However, he has also begun asking me lots of questions again: 'Would Mummy and you still be together if you had not met Jenny?' 'Why did you leave?' He has suddenly become interested in sex and is curious to see our bedroom and where I sleep. Recently when we were with my mother he said to her, 'Adults spend all night long sexing - that's why Dad is always so tired!' This reminded me of what he said to me soon after meeting Jenny: 'Have you and Jenny been making babies?'

He and I have started going swimming together. I have never liked swimming but to my surprise have really enjoyed going with him. I think that it is the physical side that I like: changing with him, having a shower, larking around in the water together. He has also enjoyed it hugely and wants to go most times I see him now. I realise that it is the physical, day-to-day things that I miss most: seeing him asleep in bed, watching him in the bath, reading to him or with him and so on. It was really good seeing him so much over half-term and having him around the house so much. He has now put up some posters in his bedroom, which I like: sometimes I go in there and look at the posters and it gives me a sense of his presence in the house. He gets on quite well now with Roger and Rachel and he seems to be relaxed around the house.

I am aware that I have not written anything about being divorced. In fact, Teressa and I were divorced some time in 1994; I do not know exactly when. I think this ignorance is partly because the whole process is so impersonal that it is hard to know that it has happened; and partly because it is hard and painful to think about. It may seem strange to say since I left Teressa, but it felt to me as though the whole process of divorce happened too quickly and too early. As with most things, Jenny and Adrian are doing it differently and will divorce after two years' separation. In many ways this seems much better. I have lots of feelings of sadness about being divorced and find it hard to talk about. I am aware that when I meet new people I feel awkward and hope that they will not ask me too much about my private life. 'I am divorced' still feels like a kind of stigma and something to be kept hidden. I also feel a kind of disorientation at times. Recently somebody asked me where I live. I had to stop and think for several seconds before being able to reply. Similarly, I find there are times when I suddenly assume that I am going back to Essex (where I used to live). Maybe there have been so many changes over the past few years that it is taking me time to adjust. And my feeling about divorce is that if it happens too quickly it does not allow time for the necessary mourning to take place.

Re-reading some of what I have written over the past few months makes me realise how much I have moved on; much of it no longer seems relevant or appropriate now. I am beginning to realise some of the positives of life in a stepfamily. In many ways I enjoy living with Roger and Rachel: I enjoy their humour, energy, irreverence, etc. and I think they are good for me. Thomas, who is an only child, enjoys the noise, banter and arguments at meal times. I am sure that he will increasingly benefit from being part of a very different family. I also think that Roger and Rachel benefit from me and my relationship with their mum, which is very different from their parents' relationship. All of us are being opened up to new, different relationships which could potentially be very beneficial. We are being given new ideas about families, how adults relate to each other, distribution of roles and many other things.

We are approaching the second anniversary of the beginning of our relationship. It is curiously a time of both celebration and sadness - celebration because of my love for Jenny and the many wonderful things about our relationship; and sadness because of the loss and pain for everyone involved, and especially for Thomas and Teressa. I am torn between the two feelings. Sometimes I feel like rejoicing and celebrating; and at other times I am overwhelmed by sadness and do not feel at all like celebrating. It also feels as though the celebrations have to be a private affair. At the weekend we are going out with some friends of Jenny's, whom she has known for years. However, they remain good friends with Adrian and so it would not feel comfortable or appropriate to celebrate with them. There is also the fact that the early days of our relationship were shrouded in secrecy so Jenny and I are the only people who know when our relationship 'began'. One of the attractions of getting married is that it would form a more legitimate and public focus for celebration.

I can't remember having any of these thoughts last year; indeed, I can't even remember whether we celebrated our anniversary. Maybe it all felt too close to the event last year. This year I feel much more as though I am remembering and reliving some of the painful experiences of the past few years.

April 1995

On-going life . . . the last few weeks have taught me again the need for Jenny and I to keep some separate time for ourselves. It has been a very busy time. Peter is home from university. Although I like Peter and get on well with him, I find it difficult when he comes home. Partly this is because Roger and Rachel get on better with Peter than with each other. When Peter is home there is a lot more merriment and banter, the house becomes noisier and more disorganised, and it seems to me much more like the children's home than ours. Somehow it feels as though the children are in control when Peter is home. He also keeps very different hours to the rest of us: often he will go out when we are going to bed and get up around lunchtime.

Another factor has been that Jenny has been under considerable pressure at work and has been tired and run down. The last few years have had a high cost for her: she has experienced far more criticism than me and has found this hard to handle. She has lost several good friends and been rejected by Adrian's family, whom she has been close to for over 20 years. I find it extraordinary how people who have known and liked her for so many years can cut her off completely. Finally, and perhaps most sadly, her brother, her only surviving close relative, also seems to have rejected her. She has been really upset by all this and, together with the pressures of work, has been very stressed. Rachel picks up very quickly on her mother's moods and in turn becomes more demanding if Jenny is feeling low. Also Adrian continues not to make life easy and the children's contact with him remains totally unpredictable and subject to change at the last minute. What I find hard is that Jenny and I have no predictable, guaranteed time together when we know we will be undisturbed.

I notice that when we are not getting time together on our own I find it much more difficult to share Jenny with her children. I have found myself getting angry with Rachel when she has been making demands and I get irritated if Jenny spends a lot of time with them. When we are spending time together on our own I can cope with this much better. Really I would like to be able to say to the children once a week: 'Jenny and I need some time on our own together and we want you to clear out of the house for four hours.' However, Jenny feels uncomfortable about saying this (as I think I would), feeling as though that would be kicking them out of their home. Last night we left the kids to clear up after the meal and went out for a walk together - this felt really good and I was able to handle it much better when we got back and they started making demands on Jenny. No doubt Jenny feels pulled in lots of different directions.

Easter 1995

I am writing this on Easter Monday. The kids are over at Adrian's and Jenny is gardening. It feels good to have the house to myself and to have some peace and quiet. Although I now enjoy Peter, Roger and Rachel in many ways, it always feels wonderful when they are away and we have time on our own.

I miss Thomas particularly strongly at times like Easter. I looked after him for four days last week, which was really great. We spent hours in the garden playing cricket together. The only problem with seeing him so much is that I miss him more when I am not seeing him. Somehow festivals like Christmas and Easter emphasise my missing him and it hits harder.

On Saturday the family dog, Toby, was put down. It was a sad time and everyone was really upset. Jenny commented afterwards that it is sharing experiences like that which make us into a family. Yesterday was Rachel's 14th birthday. She spent the morning here and they all went over to Adrian's at lunchtime. I find birthdays a bit easier now and I feel quite flattered that the kids now seem to accept me as being part of it all.

I am fond of Rachel although I find her difficult at times. She can change very quickly from being completely selfish and self-absorbed one minute to being immensely sensitive and intuitive the next. I think she feels responsible for Adrian and worries about him; there are times when there seems to be a conflict between what she would like to do and what Adrian wants her to do. Roger does not seem to have the same conflict or feel the same sense of responsibility to Adrian.

Thomas has been in a reflective mood again this week, asking me and Jenny when were the happiest and saddest days of our lives. He told Jenny that his saddest time was the day I left and the happiest the day he was given his Sega Megadrive! He seems to need to talk about it all again. It hurts me to recognise how much he has been affected by it all. While I know it is good that he can talk about it, another part of me is frustrated that he is still talking about it after nearly two years. He has been less angry with me lately and very affectionate, which feels good. He has also been talking a lot more to Jenny and seems to be more accepting of her. He gets on extremely well with Peter, who is excellent with him and Thomas thinks he is wonderful. Roger is much more indifferent and really just tolerates Thomas.

Bang! Peace is shattered. Peter and Roger have come back early (fortunately we were not in bed!). This always happens. I am pissed off and really do not want to see them. It seems that they and Adrian are completely unable to make a plan and stick to it. Part of the problem is that they use this house as a base from which they go out to see their mates (Jenny occasionally says that they use this place as a hotel). They don't seem able to use Adrian's house in the same way and feel that they have to hang around being with him. They are going out later this evening to see their mates - but why can't they do this from Adrian's house? There is no reason why not, apart from Adrian's unhappiness about their using his house in this way. It seems to me that they see Adrian's house as a place to visit rather than a home or a place they can use as they want to. For myself, I really wish that Adrian lived further away, then they would not be able to come back here at short notice the way they do.

October 1995

It is quite a few months since I last wrote anything. Partly this is because I began a new job in April and have been extremely busy and pressurised; partly, also, I think I am more relaxed here, so do not feel quite the same need to write. I am aware that the main reason I have kept this diary has been because it has been so helpful for me.

A lot has happened over the past six months. First, Teressa has started 'seeing' someone. Thomas had hinted about it several times so I was not surprised when she told me. He also seemed to be relieved that I knew and that we could talk about it. One effect of this has been that Teressa has been much friendlier with me. She is much happier in herself and has been less angry and aggressive with me. This in turn seems to have freed Thomas. In the past he would change when I dropped him off at home. From being friendly and affectionate he would become stroppy and rude. Now he is openly affectionate with me in front of Teressa. He has also now started to say that he wants to see me more often; maybe he needed to feel that his mum was OK before he could say this.

I have mixed feelings about this new fellow: part of me feels glad that Thomas will have another man around; from a personal point of view I also recognise that I might benefit. The happier Teressa is the more reasonable she is with me, and if they marry that would be good news from a financial point of view. However, there is another part of me that feels a bit threatened: this man now sees much more of Thomas than I do and, at least to begin with, Thomas talked about him very enthusiastically. He is apparently a good cricketer and Thomas used to bore me with tales of his latest match-winning innings. One day while I was bowling to him in the garden Thomas told me that Richard could spin the ball much more than me! Several times after that I found myself practising spinning a ball and there is no doubt that I feel quite competitive with this man.

I have also been aware of this competitiveness in relation to Adrian. Jenny and Adrian are still not divorced and it feels to me as though Adrian is trying to hang on to Jenny. Recently she and I were invited to one of her friends' 50th birthday party. This man is also a good friend of Adrian's. Interestingly, both Peter and Rachel assumed that we would not be going, as I have not met Adrian and he has told his kids that he has no wish to meet me. However, Jenny was clear that she wanted to go, thereby arousing considerable anxiety in Peter and Rachel. A week before the party Adrian telephoned me. He immediately said, 'I hear that you are planning to go to my best friend's 50th birthday party.' I replied that his best friend had invited me. He went on to say that he had deliberately not had any contact with me over the previous two and a half years because he had felt so angry with me he would have hit me. He claimed I had intervened in his marriage at a time when Jenny had been very vulnerable and open to exploitation. This made me realise that, while I feel considerable guilt over my own marriage, I feel no guilt in relation to Jenny's - I know that she would have left him one day even if I had never shown up.

Adrian went on to tell me how devastated he felt about what had happened and how he hated the fact that I live in 'his' house with his children. He made it clear that he puts most of the blame for what happened at my door. I have been feeling frustrated that he and I have not met, thinking that it leads to the kids feeling that they have to protect Adrian from me. So I suggested we meet in a pub on the Thursday evening before the party (I think I am also curious to meet him). He agreed to meet, and said he did not know what he was doing on Thursday but he would confirm it with me. Thursday evening came with no word from Adrian, so I assumed he had changed his mind. Jenny and I settled down to watch a film together. At 9.15 p.m. the phone rang and it was Adrian, asking if we were still on to meet. I replied that I had started to do something else and that I was not coming out now. He became quite angry and said that I was going back on our agreement.

I felt angry about this and it made me understand a bit more what happens over contact. Previously I could never understand why it always seems so complex for Adrian to arrange to see his kids. The children have a vague idea that they might be seeing their dad but are never concrete or clear. What seems to happen is that because Adrian's work is of such national importance he can never commit himself in advance. When he is finally free, he rings the kids. However, in the meantime they have often started something else. Because they are so aware of his vulnerability they usually fit in around him. It leaves me with a sense of anger that he assumes that his time is so much more important than anyone else's.

In the event he and I spent the party avoiding each other. Jenny is now saying that she wants me to meet him. She thinks he is still clinging on to some idealised notion of her and is denying the reality that their marriage is over. Her feeling is that all the time we do not meet it is colluding with his denial. I certainly feel very frustrated with Adrian and am angry that he talks to the children about his pain so much. It is as though he has stopped being a father and is asking them to take care of him. It must put them in a difficult position and they are remarkably friendly with me, given that he apparently tells them what a shit I am. I also think that the fact that he will not let go of Jenny makes it harder for the kids to move on.

I also feel frustrated because Jenny and I have been talking of getting married next summer - clearly this depends on the divorce being finalised. I am aware that Adrian has a very powerful influence on all of us, which I resent. He travels abroad on business a lot. Although they would not admit it, my sense is that the kids are also relieved when he is away.

I am aware that I sound quite bitter. I think in part this is because I feel powerless in many areas of my life. This week is half-term. I had arranged with Teressa that I would have Thomas for three days. However, at the last minute she changed her plans and Thomas has now gone to his grandparents in Essex for the week. I still find it difficult to get angry with Teressa (perhaps because of my guilt) and I have been taking my anger out on Jenny. We both have difficulty in getting angry with our ex-partners; what tends to happen is that Jenny gets furious about Teressa's behaviour and I get mad with Adrian.

I am suddenly feeling desperately sad about a lot of things. I am missing Thomas terribly and hate it when I go a long while without seeing him. Tonight I watched a film (*Nell* with Jodie Foster) and to my surprise I found myself feeling really sad and upset that Jenny and I cannot have a child. I have this sense of wanting to create a child of our own, whom we both love and do not have to share with anyone else. I think some of my bitterness is because life feels so complicated and because as a family we are dependent on people who, at best, do not always want to make life easy for Jenny and me.

I also still find being a stepfather really hard. Somewhere deep inside me there is a voice which says that a man's role is to be the head of the family: the man should be in charge and the final authority. The fact that I do not fulfil this role, that I live in Jenny's house, that she is much wealthier than I am, that I do not have a parental role in relation to Roger and Rachel, that Jenny is such a strong personality and very much 'in charge' in this house - all these facts leave me feeling quite powerless and impotent. Traditional gender roles simply do not work in stepfamilies, especially if the children are teenagers. However, this leaves me struggling to understand what my role is and how I fit into things. It poses the question for me of how to feel good about myself as a man. I think that I also feel undermined by Adrian's comments to me that I have no right to live in 'his' house with his children. The fact that he talks to the children about his feelings regarding me adds to my insecurity.

This morning I was talking to Jenny in bed about some of these feelings. After a while we started having an argument about money and she called me Adrian by mistake. After I had got over my fury, the irony of it seemed very funny. However, it was also a graphic reminder of some of the shadows hanging over our relationship.

Jenny and I have also had to adjust to changes in our relationship. When we were first together there was a madness about how we felt about each other. There was a time when I would have taken extraordinary risks just to spend half an hour with her. Sometimes I feel sad that this madness has calmed down. I recognise that this is inevitable and that life could not have carried on as it was; for the first few months of our relationship I did hardly any work at all and it completely took over my life. Jenny has recently commented that she is glad we can now spend an evening together reading, and that in our early passionate days she used to look forward to the time when we would be a boring couple! We have also had to realise that we are both complex people, with many wounds from the past. During the early stages of our relationship the excitement and 'madness' gave us enormous energy and zest. Now we are having to come to terms with the fact that our energy levels are much lower and we are both tired after the events of the past few years. What is exciting is that we seem to be able to recapture some of these feelings of love when we are sufficiently relaxed, for instance on holiday.

Rachel is going through a difficult stage at the moment. She and Jenny are similar in personality and are clashing a lot. At times it feels as though they only have to look at each other to start arguing. I know that Jenny feels exhausted by what she sees as Rachel's constant criticisms of her. Jenny tells me that she was a very angry, disruptive teenager (which I can believe!). What is not clear is how much Rachel's anger is connected to her parents' separation and how far it is a normal adolescent process. The danger is that Jenny's guilt sometimes tells her that it is the former and this makes it more difficult for her to handle the situation. Jenny sometimes uses me as a sounding board about how difficult she finds Rachel. However, if I ever criticise Rachel, Jenny immediately leaps to her defence and tells me how intolerant I am being! To be fair, I don't like Jenny saying anything remotely critical about Thomas.

It seems important that Jenny and I work through our anger and bitterness in relation to our ex-partners. While we feel angry with them it is all too easy to lay any problems at their door. I have come to learn that it is hard to feel good about myself if I feel so critical and hostile towards my father. I need to make peace with the memory of him. In the same way, it is hard to feel really good about Thomas if I am so angry with his mother. When Rachel is being a pain I sometimes find myself thinking 'that's her father in her causing her to behave like that'. You can end up hating the child because they remind you of the other parent. Perhaps part of the desire for Jenny and I to have a child is because of the fantasy that any child of ours will obviously be wonderful, perfect and without fault! (Unlike our children who at times carry the unwanted memory of Adrian and Teressa.)

It is interesting to think about Jenny's relationship with Rachel. They fight a lot and can both be very aggressive with each other. Rachel can be extremely critical of her mother. At the same time, it feels to me as though Rachel is very envious of Jenny. She is always taking her clothes to wear; she complains bitterly if Jenny buys herself anything new and thinks that she should also be entitled to new clothes; and recently when Jenny had two days off work she predictably had the following day off school. I can remember saying to Jenny that Rachel seems envious of her and wants whatever she has. Jenny's flippant response was to say, 'Well, she's not having you!'

Thinking about sexuality makes me think that, while I am aware of some of Rachel's friends' emerging sexuality, I find it difficult to think of Rachel's sexuality - presumably because it does not feel safe. I don't think that she sees me in remotely sexual terms either (whereas she and her friends seem to compete over who can be the most flirtatious with their fathers). Jenny sometimes gets annoyed if I comment about any of Rachel's friends' attractiveness. Her usual remark is that Rachel is much more attractive than any of them! Sexuality is very complex in stepfamilies. Perhaps somewhere there is a kind of very primitive feeling that anything of Jenny's is also mine. Rachel is very like her mum in lots of ways and I sometimes look at her and wonder if Jenny was like that when she was 14. Occasionally looking at Rachel I feel really sad that Jenny and I met when we were in our forties. Maybe sexual abuse in stepfamilies is partly an unconscious attempt to connect with a part of one's partner that one never knew and is now lost.

I can also remember having several very vivid and erotic dreams about Thomas shortly after I left. These dreams frightened me at the time. Now they seem to be more to do with my wish to reconnect with him at a time when I felt very out of touch.

Jenny has just read all that I have written. She thinks that it is one long whinge and that anyone reading it would be put off stepfamily life for ever. I think that this 'diary' reflects the fact that I have used it for myself and for my own 'therapy'. Inevitably, it is full of the problems of the past 18 months and it does not reflect the many good, happy times - I have not felt the need to write about them in the same way.

January 1996

We have spent our second Christmas together as a stepfamily. Things that annoyed me last year (such as the decorations) did not seem to be a problem at all this year. My mother came and stayed for a couple of days over Christmas, which was really good. The kids accepted her and were very friendly with her. Some of my family came over on Boxing Day. They all get on well with Jenny and like her. Their presence made me feel good and as though I belong here much more.

Another positive thing is that Thomas is now staying regularly. He seems much more ready to leave his mum now, presumably because he does not feel that he has to worry about her so much. He stayed with us on New Year's Eve. It was the first time that he had stayed up until midnight and he was really excited. I enjoyed the evening and it was great to share that experience with him. Having him stay regularly makes a huge difference to me - I feel much more involved with him and his life. He is also getting on really well now with Jenny's kids and they have started arguing and squabbling together in a normal way.

Generally life as a stepfamily is beginning to feel much easier. The bottom line is that it has been hard for me to learn to live with someone else's kids. Although I am fond of them all as individuals, I never feel totally relaxed when they are in the house. I have needed regular breaks away from them when I could be on my own with Jenny. I am sure they would also say that it has been hard to accept and live with a stranger. However, I now feel much more optimistic about the future. Jenny and I are talking of getting married in the summer, which is an exciting thought. I live with the woman I love: someone who infuriates, frustrates and surprises me, but who loves me and has done me an enormous amount of good. I do not regret what I have done. I am happier than at any time in my life. Whatever the pain to other people and to me, I know that what I have done has been the right thing for me.

Afterword

So does keeping a diary help a difficult situation? Certainly Leslie felt that it did. I suggested it to Leslie with a view to giving him some self power to combat his helplessness in the situation in which he found himself, but which he had also created. So it was difficult for him to blame anyone but himself, or perhaps Jenny and thus jeopardise the happiness which he had belatedly found.

Some people have found that writing letters to an abusive parent, although not necessarily sending them, has helped them come to terms with what happened to them in their childhood, when they were powerless to prevent it. For some, perhaps notably those who are literate and enjoy creating a therapeutic space for the self, they can be enabled to objectify and then reintegrate a different perspective of a current family situation. Although the success of the Open University in providing opportunities for self education would belie this apparent exclusivity. Indeed a recent series of articles in the Guardian (19th March 1996) commends this form of self therapy including the use of Net Support groups in the Internet. How about an Internet Supporting Stepfamily Group to complement the work of the Stepfamily Telephone Counselling Service with whose inauguration I was involved some ten years ago? Many of us are now semi-computer literate, and for those that aren't it might possibly improve relationships with stepchildren if they can instruct their stepparent and begin a relationship through the relative objectivity of the word processor.

Margaret Robinson

Useful Books

A list of over 50 books specifically selected on stepfamily issues for step-parents and parents, and another list of over 60 books for children together with a selective annotated bibliography for those working with stepfamilies are available from the National Stepfamily Association. Some of these may be hard to obtain and some are out of print but most should be available through your library.

There are only a few books about stepfatherhood, for example, in *"Father over Forty, Becoming an older father"* there is a chapter on stepfatherhood. Many of the general step-parenting books mention stepfathering and the National Stepfamily Association has a booklet mentioned below. However, there are several now appearing on fatherhood after divorce, some of which also explore stepfatherhood, such as *Dad's Place* by Jill Burrett.

For the stepfather who has never been a parent, there are many books on parenting but, again, little awareness of the impact of parenting a ready made ten year old. *"The Parents Book, getting on well with our children"* is good on building relationships which many stepfathers may find helpful.
(I Sokolov and D Hutton, 1988. Thorsons).

All books published by the National Stepfamily Association and other selected items are available by mail order, and some key ones are listed below.

A Baby of our own, A new baby in a stepfamily (1993) Erica De'Ath
Another Step: Weddings in stepfamilies (1995) Kathleen Cox
Parenting Threads, Caring for Children when Couples part (1992) Erica De'Ath and Dee Slater

Stepping into Stepfathering (1995) Stephen Kaye
To and Fro Children, A guide to successful parenting after divorce
 (1993) Jill Burrett
Where there's a will, there's a way: Making a Will in a stepfamily
 (1993) Imogen Clout

Tapes
Audio tapes also available from STEPFAMILY: *Teenagers and Stepfamilies,* and *Teenagers and Divorce* produced by the Trust for the Study of Adolescence.

Useful Addresses
For informal advice and support

Exploring Parenthood
4 Ivory Place
Treadgold Street
London W11 4BP
Tel: 0171 221 6681

Families Need Fathers
(National Admin. Centre)
134 Curtain Road
London EC2A 3AR
Tel: 0171 613 5060

Gingerbread,
16-17 Clerkenwell Close
London EC1R 0AA
England Advice Line:
0171 336 8184
Wales Advice Line:
01792 648 728

Grandparents Federation,
Moot House, The Stow
Harlow, Essex
CM20 3AG
Tel: 01279 444964

Home-Start UK,
2 Salisbury Road,
Leicester LE7 7QR
Tel: 01533 554988
Fax: 01533 549323

Mothers Apart From Their
Children (MATCH)
c/o BM Problems,
London WC1N 3XX

Network of Contact and
Access Centres
St Andrews with Castlegate
URC, Goldsmith Street
Nottingham NG1 5JT
0115 948 4557

National Council For One
Parent Families
255 Kentish Town Road
London NW5 2LX
Tel: 0171 267 1361

National Stepfamily
Association
3rd Floor, Chapel House
18 Hatton Place
London EC1N 8RU
Helpline: 0990 168 388
Tel: 0171 209 2460
Fax: 0171 209 2461

One Parent Families
Scotland
13 Gayfield Square
Edinburgh EH1 3NX
Tel: 0131 556 3899

Parent Network
44-46 Caversham Road
London NW5 2DS
Tel: 0171 485 8535
Fax: 0171 267 4426

Parentline
Westbury House
57 Hart Road, Thundersley
Essex SS7 3PP
Helpline: 01268 757077
Fax: 01268 757039

Soldiers' Sailors' And
Airmen's Families
Association (SSAFA)
19 Queen Elizabeth St.
London SE1 2LP
Tel: 0171 403 8783

Stepfamily Scotland
5 Coates Place
Edinburgh EH3 7AA
Office 0131 225 8005
Helpline 0131 225 5800

For counselling or therapy

Asian Family Counselling
Service,
74 The Avenue, West
Ealing, London W13 8LB
Tel: 0181 997 5749

Catholic Marriage Care,
23 Kensington Square,
London W8 5HN
Tel: 0171 937 3781

Institute for Family Therapy
43 New Cavendish Street
London W1M 7RG
Tel: 0171 935 1651

Jewish Marriage Council
23 Ravenshurst Avenue
London NW4 4EE
Tel: 0181 203 6311
Tel. Advice: 0181 203 6314
Helpline: 0345 581 999

London Marriage Guidance
Council
76a New Cavendish St.
Corner of Harley Street
London W1M 7LB
Tel: 0171 580 1087

National Council For The
Divorced and Separated
13 High Street,
Little Shelford
Cambridgeshire CB2 5ES
Tel: 0116 2700 595

RELATE, Marriage
Guidance
Herbert Gray College
Little Church Street, Rugby
Warwickshire CV21 3AP
Tel: 01788 573 241
Fax: 01788 575 007

Westminster Pastoral
Foundation
23 Kensington Square
London W8 5HN
Tel: 0171 937 6956

For mediation

Family Mediation Scotland
127 Rose Street,
South Lane
Edinburgh EH2 4BB
Tel: 0131 220 1610

Family Mediators
Association
PO Box 2028, Hove
East Sussex BN3 3HU
Tel: 01273 747 750

National Family Mediation
9 Tavistock Place
London WC1H 9SN
Tel: 0171 383 5993
Fax: 0171 383 5994

For legal advice

Children's Legal Centre,
The University of Essex
Wivenhoe Park
Colchester CO4 3SQ
Tel: 01206 873 820

National Association of
Citizens Advice Bureaux
Myddleton House
115-123 Pentonville Rd.
London, N1 9LZ
Tel: 0171 833 2181

Child Support Agency,
Room 209, Quay House
The Waterfront
Brierley Hill
West Midlands DY5 1XZ
Tel: 01384 574882
National Enquiry Line:
0345 133 133
Employers Enquiry Line:
0345 134 134
Child Support Literature
Line: 0345 830 830

Solicitors Family Law
Association,
PO Box 302, Orpington
Kent BR6 8QX
Tel: 01689 850 227

For general social security,
benefits and welfare advice
The telephone directory,
Town Hall or library can
direct you to your local:
Citizens Advice Bureau,
Legal Advice Centre, Social
Security Dept.

For a free information pack which includes a membership leaflet, examples of our newsletters for adults and children, details of forthcoming conferences and training events and a publications leaflet showing the full range of books and booklets answering questions on:

- changing children's family names
- teenagers
- stepmothering
- financial planning
- stepparent adoption
- Christmas celebrations
- parental responsibility
- grandparents
- weddings
- stepfathering
- making a will
- a new baby
- holidays
- contact

Write sending a self addressed C5 envelope to the address below.

Please send me

☐ an information pack
☐ how to become a volunteer telephone counsellor
☐ more information on donating to STEPFAMILY

Name ....

Address ....

.... Postcode ....

Please return this form to:

National Stepfamily Association, 3rd Floor, Chapel House
18 Hatton Place, London EC1N 8RU
Tel: 0171 209 2460   Fax: 0171 209 2461

There is also a Helpline if you want to ask your questions direct
0990 168 388 Monday to Friday 2-5 or 7-10pm

Registered Charity No. 1005351   Company Limited by guarantee 2552166